THE SECRET WORLD OF

Bees

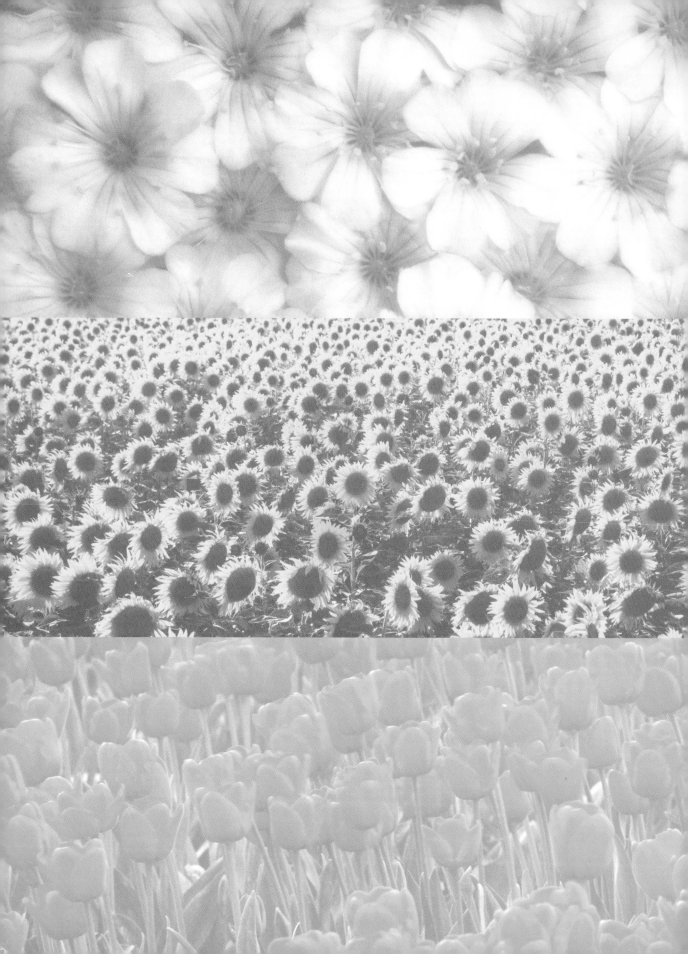

THE SECRET WORLD OF

Bees

Malcolm Penny

Chicago, Illinois

Project Editors: Geoff Barker, Marta Segal Block, Sarah Jameson, Jennifer Mattson
Production Manager: Brian Suderski
Consultants: Michael Chinery, J. Christopher Brown
Illustrated by Stuart Lafford
Designed by Ian Winton
Picture research by Vashti Gwynn
Planned and produced by Discovery Books

Library of Congress Cataloging-in-Publication Data:
Penny, Malcolm.
Bees / Malcolm Penny.
v. cm. -- (The secret world of)
Includes bibliographical references and index.
Contents: What are bees? -- The life cycle of a honeybee -- Bees as builders -- Life in honeybee city -- Bee senses -- Finding and sharing food -- Enemies of bees -- Humans and honey.
ISBN 0-7398-7019-X (lib. bdg.)
1. Bees--Juvenile literature. [1. Bees. 2. Honeybee.] I. Title. II. Series.
QL565.2.P46 2004
595.79'9--dc21
                    2003002241

Printed and bound in the United States by Lake Book Manufacturing, Inc.
07 06 05 04 03   10 9 8 7 6 5 4 3 2 1

Acknowledgments
The publishers would like to thank the following for permission to reproduce photographs:
p. 8 Anthony Bannister/Natural History Photographic Agency; p. 9 Michael Fogden/Oxford Scientific Films; pp. 10, 24, 26 Kim Taylor/Bruce Coleman Collection; pp. 11, 20, 30 Ken Preston-Mafham/Premaphotos Wildlife; p.13 Natural Selection Inc./Bruce Coleman Collection; p.14 Sir Jeremy Grayson/Bruce Coleman Collection; p.16 David Thompson/Oxford Scientific Films; pp. 15, 17, 22, 27, 41 Scott Camazine/Oxford Scientific Films; p.18 Mr. J. Brackenbury/Bruce Coleman Collection; p.19 Breck P. Kent/Animals Animals/Oxford Scientific Films; p.21 Dr. Derek Bromhall/Oxford Scientific Films; pp. 23, 38 Treat Davidson/Frank Lane Picture Agency; p.28 N.A. Callow/Natural History Photographic Agency; p. 29 (right and left): Robert Pickett/Ecoscene; pp. 32-33, 43 Stephen Dalton/Natural History Photographic Agency; p. 36 Simon Trevor/SAL/Oxford Scientific Films; p.37 Martin Garwood/Natural History Photographic Agency; p.39: Nigel J. Dennis/Natural History Photographic Agency; p.42 David Woodfall/Natural History Photographic Agency.

Other Acknowledgments
Cover photograph: Stephen Dalton/Natural History Photographic Agency

Every effort has been made to contact copyright holders of any material reproduced in this book. Any omissions will be rectified in subsequent printings if notice is given to the publisher.

Note to the Reader
Some words are shown in bold, **like this.** You can find out what they mean by looking in the glossary.

Contents

CHAPTER 1
What Are Bees?

Bees belong to the *Hymenoptera* order, or group, of animals, which also includes wasps and ants.

There are more than 25,000 different kinds of bees.

The largest bees are 1.5 in. (4 cm) long, and the smallest are less than 0.1 in. (2 mm) long.

The buzzing sound made by flying bees comes from their wings beating about 190 times every second.

Bees are found wherever there are flowering plants. They live on all the continents of the world except Antarctica.

Bees are insects, and like all insects, they have jointed legs, an outer skeleton, and a body that is divided into three sections. The head has jaws and a sucking tube for drinking nectar from flowers. There are two pairs of feelers on the head. The smaller pair, called the palps, are used for handling and tasting food, and the longer, usually thinner pair are the **antennae,** used mainly for smelling (or tasting) the bee's surroundings.

The middle part of the bee's body is called the **thorax,** which has two pairs of wings and three pairs of legs attached to it. The rear part of the body is the **abdomen.** It contains internal body parts such as the heart and the **honey stomach,** the structure that helps the bee store and carry nectar.

Like the wings of other insects, bees' wings are made of a transparent substance called **chitin.** A bee has two wings on each side. The back wings are smaller than the front ones. As a bee flies, powerful muscles in the thorax move the wings up and down. The wing tips twist slightly in flight, helping to push the bee forward through the air.

Like all other insects, a bee's body is made up of three parts: the head, the thorax, and the abdomen. Honeybees like this one also have special structures for carrying honey and pollen—the honey stomach and pollen baskets.

Wings
Two pairs of wings made of chitin are attached to the bee's thorax.

Compound eyes
A bee's **compound eyes** are made up of many small eyes joined together.

Antennae
The two antennae are used for smelling and tasting.

Stinger
A bee's stinger is used only in self-defense.

Palps
The palps handle and taste food.

Honey stomach
Located inside the honeybee's abdomen, the honey stomach carries nectar collected from flowers. The nectar will be made into honey.

Wax glands
Flakes of white wax for nest-building are made by special **glands** in the bee's abdomen.

Pollen basket
Stiff bristles on the back legs form the **pollen** baskets, which carry yellow pollen grains from flowers.

Tongue
A honeybee's tongue is long and slender. It is used for sucking nectar from flowers.

STEALTHY STINGERS

Bees did not appear on Earth until about 135 million years ago. They **evolved** from wasps that hunted other insects. When flowers appeared, some of these wasps turned to **pollen** and nectar for food and stopped eating insects entirely. They became bees. Like their wasp relatives, most bees are solitary, meaning that they live and search for food on their own. Some kinds of bees, however, live in colonies, or large groups.

Unlike wasps, which eat other insects and use their smooth, hollow stingers over and over again to **paralyze** their **prey,** bees do not need to hunt or sting their food. They use their stingers only for defense. The stinger of a bee (or a wasp) is developed from the egg-laying tube, called the ovipositor, and only the female bee of any **species** can sting. Male bees have no stinger at all.

While a queen honeybee has a smooth, curved stinger that can be used many times, a worker honeybee's stinger is covered with sharp spines. Once it has been used, these spines prevent it from coming out of the wound. Instead, it comes out of the bee. The stinger's poison sac comes out

Some kinds of bees have no stingers at all, whether they are male or female. These stingless bees from South Africa are striped like bees that do have stingers, so that birds are afraid to eat them.

8

as well and continues pumping venom into the victim. The bee dies, but the colony as a whole has so many members that the loss of one or two bees is not a serious problem. The black and yellow colors of wasps and some bees warn other animals that an attack might result in a painful sting.

Bees the Pollinators

The colors and scents of flowers, and the nectar they produce, are attractive to bees. When a bee visits a flower to feed, some of the flower's pollen brushes off and sticks to the bee. This orchid bee is visiting an orchid in Costa Rica. Attached to its back is pollen from the last orchid it visited. Some of the pollen will stick to this flower and **pollinate** it so it can produce seeds. Pollination (the transfer of tiny pollen grains from one flower to another) is essential for the **reproduction** of most plants.

I DIDN'T KNOW THAT

A bumblebee visits a foxglove flower, a favorite source of nectar. You can clearly see the bee's long, curved tongue. It is a very useful tool for sucking nectar from tube-shaped flowers like this one.

LONER BEES

Bumblebees and honeybees are **social** insects. They live in colonies containing hundreds or even thousands of bees, all of which work together for the good of the whole community. They are familiar creatures in our backyards.

Most kinds of bees, however, are solitary creatures and do not live in large groups. Each solitary female bee makes her own nest, usually in a **burrow,** or hole, where she uses mud, chewed wood, or leaf fragments to construct one or more little **cells.** Each cell receives an egg and a store of **pollen** and nectar. The female then seals up the nest and flies away.

The eggs hatch into wormlike **larvae** and eat the pollen and nectar in their cells, but they never see their mother. She usually dies soon after finishing her nest. Mason bees, carpenter bees, leaf-cutter bees, and mining bees are all types of solitary bees.

A BUMBLEBEE COLONY

There are about 300 different **species** of bumblebees. Most of them live in the cooler, northern parts of the world in colonies of between 50 and 600 members, only one of which is able to lay eggs. She is known as a queen.

In the springtime the queen bumblebee looks for a suitable hole in the ground in which to make her nest. She brings in pollen and forms it into a kind of loaf on which she lays her eggs. She also makes wax containers called honey-pots to store nectar. The wax comes from **glands** in her **abdomen.**

When the eggs hatch, the larvae feed on the loaf. They soon turn into adult female bees, but are smaller than their mother. They are called workers, and they gradually take over the work of collecting food and feeding younger bees. The colony continues to live in the same hole, which can be enlarged if necessary. In late summer some of the eggs develop into next year's queens. The queen also lays some eggs that have not been **fertilized.** These grow into male bumblebees. When the new queens become adults, they fly out and mate. The males and the year-old queen die, and the new queens **hibernate** until the following spring, when the cycle starts all over again.

In this bumblebee nest, the worker bees are busy filling the honey-pots and feeding younger bees. You can see a full honey-pot near the top left of the picture.

11

HONEY FOR ALL SEASONS

Unlike bumblebee colonies, honeybee colonies go on from year to year, surviving the coldest winters. A honeybee colony, or hive, can survive for 30 years or more and may contain as many as 100,000 bees at any one time. Three types of bee live in a honeybee colony: the queen, who lays all the eggs; the workers, or small female bees that do all the work; and male **drones,** whose only job is to mate with new queens. Though honeybees and bumblebees both produce honey, honeybee nests are much more complex than those of bumblebees. Honeybees build nests with wax sheets called **combs,** each of which contains thousands of neat, six-sided **cells.**

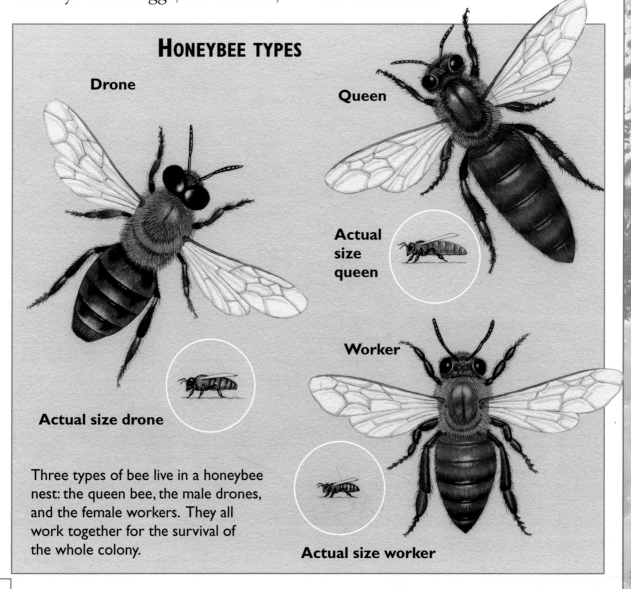

HONEYBEE TYPES

Drone

Queen

Actual size queen

Actual size drone

Worker

Actual size worker

Three types of bee live in a honeybee nest: the queen bee, the male drones, and the female workers. They all work together for the survival of the whole colony.

Honeybees gather in large numbers at a nest in Colorado. All the bees here are workers and the queen is buried somewhere in the middle. The drones have not yet hatched.

CHAPTER 2
The Life Cycle of a Honeybee

Bees have four stages in their life cycle. They start as an egg, which then hatches into a **larva**. The larva becomes a **pupa**, which finally turns into an adult. This remarkable process of change is called **metamorphosis.**

These bees have left their old nest in a swarm and will soon start to build a new nest. Groups of worker bees will fly out to find a suitable nesting site, often choosing a hollow tree or an old barn.

A queen honeybee can lay as many as 2,000 eggs in a single day. However, she cannot start a colony, collect food, or produce wax by herself. She cannot even feed herself. Instead, she relies on the worker bees to do these things for her.

A worker larva is fed over 100 meals each day and grows to as many as 300 times its original weight before it starts to make the change into an adult bee.

Most worker bees live for about five weeks. Drones live for several months, while queens can live for up to six years.

A NEW QUEEN

When a honeybee colony becomes too crowded, the queen flies away with a **swarm** of worker bees. Inside the nest they left, the remaining worker bees begin to rear new queens in specially enlarged cells. The larvae in these cells are given an especially rich food called **royal jelly** that ensures they will grow into new queens and not workers.

The first new queen to hatch crawls around to all the other

A queen honeybee lays an egg into an empty cell. She is the large, unstriped bee in the center, surrounded by some of her workers.

special cells containing unhatched queens. With the help of workers, she kills the developing queen pupae with her stinger. She then flies out of the nest to mate with a number of **drones.** The drones die after mating, but the new queen returns to the nest. From now on, she will lay all of the colony's eggs in the nest, which will be tended by the workers.

FROM EGG TO ADULT

1. The queen honeybee lays an egg in a clean, empty cell. 2. A nurse bee feeds and cleans the larva when it hatches. 3. The fully grown larva becomes a pupa. 4. Inside the pupa case, the larva changes shape and becomes an adult bee. 5. Finally, the new winged adult honeybee crawls out of the cell to begin its life in the nest.

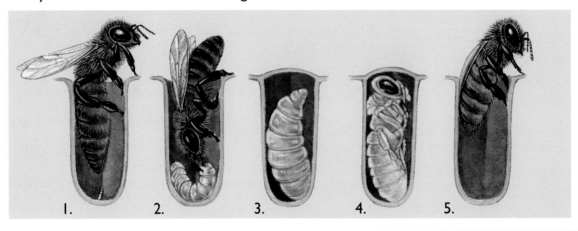

1.　　2.　　3.　　4.　　5.

EGGS AND LARVAE

A honeybee's egg hatches in three days to produce a **larva,** which is small, white, and wormlike. For the first few days, workers called nurse bees feed the larvae with **royal jelly,** a white, creamy substance they produce from **glands** in their head. After that, the larvae are fed on **pollen** and honey from stores in the nest.

An army of honeybee larvae are growing in their cells. Two have completed the pupa stage and are beginning to emerge from their cells as adult bees.

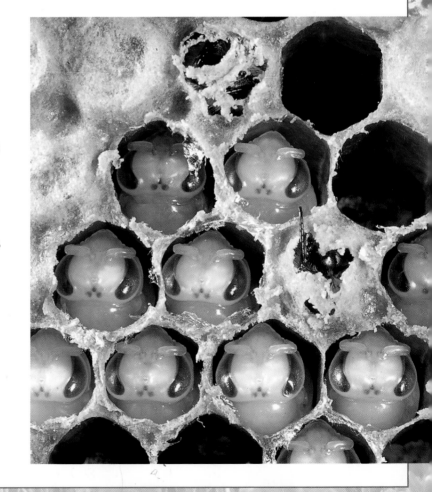

16

The nurse bees keep the larvae clean, removing droppings and any dirt that has been brought into the nest by accident. As each larva grows, its skin becomes too tight. Since the skin will not stretch, it splits and the larva grows a new skin. This process is called molting. Nurse bees remove the old skins as they are shed.

PUPATION AND ADULTHOOD

After five or six days and five molts, the larva wraps itself in a silklike substance, making a cocoon, and becomes a **pupa.** The nurse bees cover its **cell** with wax and leave the pupa to change into an adult bee. A new young worker bee is ready to leave the cell twelve days after becoming a pupa.

If a new bee is to be a queen, the adult comes out after seven days. A **drone** takes the longest to develop—fifteen days.

Although it has strong jaws, the young bee cannot make its way out of its cell alone, so other workers gather around and help it out by chewing at the wax lid.

Winter Bees

In the fall, workers block the male drones from getting to the nest's food stores. The drones must either fly off or starve inside the nest. With no drones to feed, worker bees are more likely to survive the winter on their honey stores. When winter comes, honeybees stay inside the nest because there is little or no pollen to gather from flowers. The bees do not truly **hibernate,** but spend much of their time feeding on their honey stores, like the bee in the picture below. They cluster together to keep warm, waiting for spring to come. If spring flowers open late, the whole colony can die of starvation.

I DIDN'T KNOW THAT

CHAPTER 3
Bees as Builders

Honeybees are well known for their spectacular wax **combs** made up of thousands of **cells**— but there are other, simpler constructions made by other kinds of bee.

BURROWS AND HOLES

Most solitary bees nest in a hole or **burrow** that they have made themselves, though they will often use an existing hole if they can find one that is suitable.

A wild honeybees' nest has roughly 100,000 cells in about six combs.

In order to produce a certain amount of wax, a honeybee must eat from six to ten times as much honey.

Some bees, called cuckoo bees, never build a nest at all but lay their eggs in other bees' nests. Their larvae eat the larvae in the host's nest and steal from their food stores.

▶ A mason bee is making a nest. She gathers small stones and glues them together with sticky juices from her mouth. The result is as strong as concrete.

Mason bees use their strong jaws to burrow into the mortar between bricks, or even into the bricks themselves. Their **larvae** develop inside these burrows. Some **species** use juices from their mouth to glue tiny stones together at the entrance, so that it is only just big enough for the new adult bee to squeeze through when it hatches. Mason bees have been nesting in the walls of one college in Oxford, England, for several hundred years.

Carpenter bees like this one make long burrows in dead wood. They can cause serious damage to roof timbers and the frames of houses.

Carpenter bees chew into wood to make their burrows, often making several long tunnels close together. In a dead tree lying on the forest floor, this helps speed up the natural process of rotting, returning nutrients from the tree back into the soil.

LEAF-CUTTERS

Another group of solitary bees that live in holes are the leaf-cutters. They do not dig their own holes, but look for existing holes that they can tailor for their own use. They then cut round sections from sturdy leaves—rosebush leaves are a favorite—and fit them into the hole as a lining. This creates a cozy **burrow** in which leaf-cutter bees can make **cells** (from more leaf sections) for their eggs.

A leaf-cutter bee bites a circular piece out of a rose leaf to line her nest. In the spring and summer, you can often see rose leaves with bites taken out of them by these bees.

BUILDING BEE CITY

Unlike solitary bees, honeybee colonies usually set up their homes in the trunk or branch of a large, hollow tree or sometimes in a cave.

The **swarm** of bees that has left its old, crowded nest will look for a new nesting place. Once the colony has moved into its new home, the bees' first task is to hang a vertical sheet of wax from the roof, with one edge glued to the wall. On both sides of this sheet, the workers start to build the first cells of their **comb.** The cells are built in rows, close together so that their walls touch, and they are all six-sided. This is the shape that allows the greatest number of cells to fit into the smallest space.

In a typical wild honeybees' nest, different parts of the comb have different uses. Honey and **pollen** are stored in the upper levels and

This is a wild honeybees' nest in a tree in Kenya, Africa. The comb has room to expand downward and sideways as the colony grows.

below them are the nursery cells, where the eggs and **larvae** of workers and **drones** are raised. When they are needed, the workers build a few special cells for future queens at the bottom of the comb and around the edges.

The Colony Grows

As soon as the first **cells** in the **comb** are built, the queen starts laying eggs. Until they hatch, she has only the workers she brought with her to look after the eggs, find food, and build new cells. This is a very busy time for the new colony. But within four weeks a new generation of workers appears, and more bees are born to the colony every day.

This comb has been made by killer bees—a type of African honeybee—inside a hollow tree.

The Wonders of Wax

An important factor in the success of honeybees and bumblebees is their ability to make wax. They produce wax from **glands** in their **abdomen.** You can see a tiny flake of white wax coming out from the abdomen of the worker bee below. The bee will scrape the wax flakes together with its legs and then mold them with its jaws. The wax will set into a light, firm sheet and will be used to build the cells where the eggs are laid and the food is stored. When beeswax is first produced, it is soft and nearly white. It becomes darker as it hardens.

NATURAL GLUE

While bees are **foraging,** they collect more than food. Some trees produce a sticky substance in their buds, called **propolis,** which the bees collect and use to seal the outside of the nest so that wind and water cannot get in. They also use propolis to cover over anything that is cluttering up the nest but too big for them to carry outside.

CHAPTER 4
Life in Honeybee City

In a honeybee colony, worker bees are all females produced from **fertilized** eggs. However, they do not lay their own eggs. Workers keep the nest clean, build new **cells,** feed and clean the **larvae,** guard the nest, and go out to **forage** for food.

When they first hatch, these bees work inside the nest. As they grow older, however, they

Below 57 °F (14 °C), honeybees stay clustered inside the nest. A colony can survive for several weeks at –50 °F (–46 °C).

About 40 lb (18 kg) of honey is needed to feed an average-sized colony over the winter.

Although around 100 bees in a colony might die each day, a typical nest will rarely contain more than one or two dead adults at any time, because their bodies are carried out of the nest by workers.

Nurse bees make as many as 1,300 visits a day to cells in the comb to feed and clean the developing larvae.

▶ As worker bees go about their cell-cleaning duties, two forager bees feed nectar to young bees who have not yet been outside the nest.

become forager bees and fly out of the nest to collect **pollen** and **nectar** from flowers. Individual foragers may fly up to 30 miles (48 kilometers) in a day, carrying as much as 0.003 ounces (75 milligrams) of nectar each time, which is equal to almost their entire body weight. Because they work so hard, forager bees live for only about five weeks. Bees born toward the end of the summer live longer because they spend the winter resting and waiting for spring to arrive.

Bees loaded up with pollen enter a skep, a type of artificial bee nest made of straw. Skeps were first used in the 1600s.

SANITATION

Honeybees are very clean insects. Even indoor workers fly outside the nest to release their droppings, taking with them any scraps of dirt or debris—including dead workers or larvae—that have collected in the nest. However, the **drones** are less tidy and leave their droppings in the nest for the workers to clean up.

AIR CONDITIONING

Bees developing inside the nursery **cells** in the nest may die if they get too hot. If the temperature does become too high, the workers start up the air conditioning. **Forager** bees collect water in their mouths, which they scatter around the nest, while others fan their wings to **evaporate** the water. At the nest entrance, guard bees fan fiercely, until a steady breeze of warm,

These worker bees at the entrance to this artificial nest are fanning their wings to help cool the bees inside. In hot weather, groups of five or ten workers take turns acting as fans all day, until the outside air cools down in the evening.

damp air flows out, cooling the nest inside. A honeybee colony can survive if the temperature outside gets up to 120 °F (49 °C), as long as the bees can find water to bring to the nest.

The Queen Bee

In a typical honeybee nest there is a single queen bee, 300 **drones,** 20,000 foraging workers, and 40,000 indoor workers. The queen is the mother of all the bees in the colony. She produces a chemical with a special odor, called **queen substance,** that keeps worker bees from laying eggs. This odor reaches all the bees in the nest and it helps to keep them all working together as a unit. When the queen dies or no longer produces queen substance, the workers create new queens by enlarging some cells and feeding the **larvae** already developing in them with **royal jelly.** If the old queen is still alive when a new queen is born, the old one is killed by her replacement. Worker bees dispose of her body outside the nest. This photograph shows a queen larva growing inside a special cell at the edge of the **comb.** The cell has been cut away so that the larva can be seen.

CHAPTER 5
Bee Senses

Bees cannot hear, but they have hairs on their bodies that are sensitive to vibrations in the air.

When bees meet, they touch antennae to learn more about each other and to pass on scents given off by the queen.

Bees' antennae are sensitive to the fragrences of flowers. Many flowers smell sweet in order to attract bees, which help plants to reproduce.

Honeybees and bumblebees live in the darkness of their nests for most of their lives. They need different senses from those of humans. Their **antennae** are very sensitive to many kinds of chemicals, particularly those found in **queen substance.** They can also distinguish between bees from their own nest and outsiders.

SPECIAL SIGHT

Bees have two kinds of eyes. On top of their head are three tiny, simple eyes that are sensitive to light. These eyes may help the bee see danger coming from above or behind. On each side of their head, bees have a **compound eye,** made up of several hundred separate tiny lenses, which are very sensitive to movement. These eyes are used to find food.

▶ A close-up of the head of a honeybee shows its sharp jaws, jointed antennae, and compound eyes. You can also see one of the simple eyes on top of the bee's head.

EXTRA SENSE

Honeybees have a keen sense of direction—as if they had a built-in compass. Whenever possible, they will line up the first sheet of wax in their **comb** so that it hangs in a line from north to south.

Using this special extra sense, all the honeybees in the nest are always able to know which way they are facing. This is an extremely useful ability for bees to have when building their complex wax combs in the dark.

Invisible Guides

Bees see a different range of colors than humans do. The name for all the colors that exist, from darkest blue to brightest red, is called the **color spectrum.** Bees cannot see colors at the far red end of this spectrum, but they are sensitive to a color at the other end of the spectrum called **ultraviolet,** which humans cannot see. Many flowers that look solid in color to us (like the yellow dandelion flower on the left below) actually have ultraviolet patterns that bees can detect. These patterns guide visiting bees to the flower's **pollen** and **nectar.** The picture of the dandelion flower on the right was taken using film that is sensitive to ultraviolet light. You can see the bright patterns on the dandelion's petals that guide the bees to the heart of the flower.

I DIDN'T KNOW THAT

CHAPTER 6
Finding and Sharing Food

Honey is a complex mixture of natural sugars (80 percent); water (18 percent); and pollen, minerals, vitamins, and protein (2 percent).

A single worker honeybee produces about one-twelfth of a teaspoon of honey in the course of her entire lifetime.

A whole honeybee colony can produce up to 2 lb (0.9 kg) of honey each day.

Honey lasts indefinitely once it has been capped with wax. Honey found in the tombs of Egyptian pharaohs was still good to eat, even though it was more than 3,000 years old.

Bees and flowers have **evolved** together. Because of the **pollen** and **nectar** they produce, almost every flower is attractive to some kind of bee at any time during the year. Some plants flower early in the year and some flower later. Fruit trees such as cherry, apple, and plum flower early in the spring. Vegetables like string beans flower in summer. Other plants, like chrysanthemums, flower in the fall.

Thoroughly dusted with pollen, a honeybee worker visits a dandelion flower. Individual workers collect pollen from the same types of flower for days at a time.

SWEET NECTAR

Nectar is produced by flowers in order to attract insects to **pollinate** them. It is a sweet, sugary liquid made at the base of the flower. A bee (or any other insect) wanting to drink the nectar must first push past the flower's **anthers** to reach the place where it is produced. In the process, pollen is transferred onto the visiting bee's body. When the bee lands on the next flower, some grains of pollen from the previous flower brush off onto the **stigma.** This pollinates the new flower so it can produce seeds.

FLOWER FOOD

This flower has been cut away to show how a bee feeds on the nectar with its long tongue. You can see the pollen grains that have been transferred onto the bee's body from the flower's anthers. The honeybee uses pollen baskets on its legs to carry pollen back to the nest.

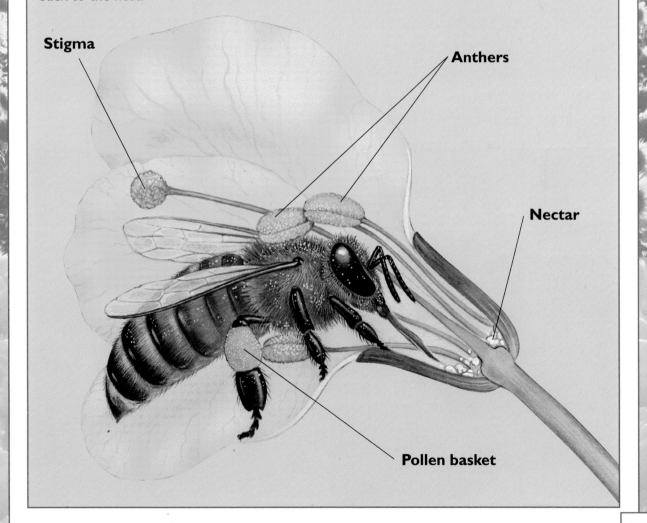

Stigma

Anthers

Nectar

Pollen basket

POLLEN CARRIERS

Forager bees have special hairs on their **abdomen** and bristles on their legs that help collect the **pollen** from flowers. They use these bristles to comb the pollen grains off of their abdomens and onto clusters of little spines on their back legs called pollen baskets. Back at the nest, the pollen that the foragers collect is stored in cells to be fed to the growing **larvae.**

Depending on the quality and quantity of nectar and pollen available, honeybees visit between 50 and 100 flowers in one trip—and sometimes up to 500 flowers.

They return to the nest with their pollen baskets stocked with orange-yellow pollen grains and their **honey stomachs** full of flower nectar. A full load of nectar in a honeybee's honey stomach fills nearly half its abdomen, which must stretch to hold it all.

HONEY MACHINES

The nectar is either eaten or made into honey and stored in **cells** around the edge of the nest. At first the nectar is a thin liquid

Her pollen baskets full, a worker honeybee uses her jaws and head to pack her cargo into a special pollen storage cell in the comb.

containing a lot of water. It has to be changed by the bees into thick honey. Some changes happen to the nectar inside the bee's honey stomach. The other changes take place after the bee **regurgitates** the liquid into the honey **cells.** The bees then fan their wings over the liquid so the water in it **evaporates** and the honey thickens up.

This busy piece of honeybee comb contains full pollen cells, honey cells (some of them capped with wax to keep them fresh), and some growing larvae.

The workers feed on nectar when it is available. The main purpose of making and storing honey is to feed the colony during the long winter months, when there is no pollen or nectar outside the nest. When a cell is full of honey, the workers carefully cap it with wax. This keeps the air out (and the honey fresh) until it is time to open up the cell and eat the honey inside.

This worker bee is covering a full honey cell with wax. This will keep the honey inside from going bad.

Dancing in the Dark

Bees can recognize landmarks around them as they fly, and they also take notice of the position of the sun. When a **foraging** honeybee finds a good source of food, it can communicate the direction, quality, and even quantity of the food supply to the other bees back at the nest. Remarkably, it does this by "dancing in the dark."

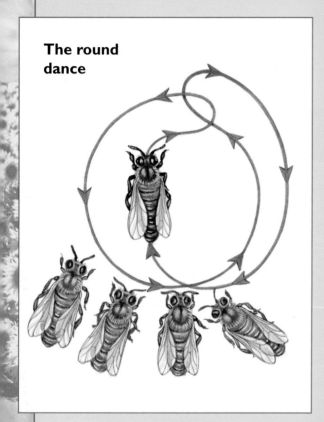

The round dance

Returning to the nest in a beeline, or straight path, the bee shares samples of a new flower's **nectar** with the others in the nest, and then performs a dance on the vertical walls of the **comb.** The dance tells the other bees all about the new source of food. The bees crowd around the dancer so that they can feel its movements in the darkness with their **antennae.**

If the food source is closer than about 250 feet (75 meters), the bee does a round dance, circling to the left and then to the right. How long and energetically the bee dances tells the other bees how rich the source of food is.

A special dance called the waggle dance is performed if the food supply is farther away. Instead of making a circle, the bee dances in a figure eight, with two loops and a straight run in the middle. During the straight run the bee waggles its **abdomen** from side to side. The direction of the straight run indicates the direction of the food source.

If the straight run goes directly upward, the source of food will be found by flying straight toward the sun. If the straight run is 45 degrees to the right of the vertical, for example, the food will be found 45 degrees to the right

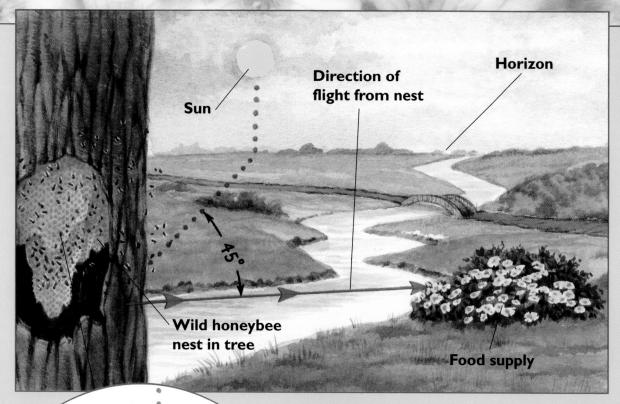

Sun

Direction of flight from nest

Horizon

45°

Wild honeybee nest in tree

Food supply

45°

The waggle dance

of the sun's position. The two diagrams on this page show how this works.

The rate at which the bee completes the straight run section of the dance tells the others how far they will have to travel.

If the food is around 350 feet (100 meters) away, the bee does the straight run about ten times in fifteen seconds. If it is around 3,500 feet (1,000 meters) away, it makes only four or five runs in the same time, and so on. Again, how energetically the dancer moves gives the other bees an idea of how good the food source is.

The other workers follow the dancer excitedly, and when they have enough information, they rush out and fly off in the right direction to find the new source of food and bring it back to the nest.

CHAPTER 7
Enemies of Bees

Some tropical bees have no stingers, but defend their nests by squirting stinging liquid at invaders.

Some spiders build their webs across the entrances to bees' nests to catch bees and other invading insects.

Dragonflies and robber flies can catch bees in midair.

▶ A honey badger feasts on the comb of a wild bees' nest in Zimbabwe, Africa. The honey tastes so good that the badger ignores the stingers of the worker bees trying to defend their nest.

Bees have many enemies, ranging in size from bears and badgers that steal their honey, to tiny mites, almost too small to see, that suck the blood of **larvae** and adult bees.

BEE HUNTERS

The risk of getting stung does not discourage some predators. Birds such as bee-eaters catch bees by the head and beat them against a twig to remove the stinger. Some lizards and toads that catch bees are not bothered by the stinger at all. Mongooses raid bees' nests and eat everything inside, including the wax **comb.** They can feel the stingers through their thick fur, but the pain does not stop them.

Even a small spider can overcome and kill a bumblebee once the bee is trapped in its sticky web and paralyzed by its poisonous bite.

INVADERS

Some animals invade bee nests in a very clever way. For example, velvet ants (which are in fact related to bees) and bee flies (which are not) are both furry, like bees, and even smell like them! Velvet ants crawl into bees' nests and lay their eggs there. When their larvae hatch, they attack and eat the young bees. Bee flies scatter their eggs near the nests of solitary bees so the fly larvae can crawl in and feed on both the bee larvae and the bees' stored food. The wax moth, sometimes called the bee moth, lays its eggs in bees' nests so that the caterpillars can eat the wax when they hatch. Bee wolves are a kind of wasp that catches bees on flowers. They **paralyze** the bees with their stinger, then carry them off to feed to their own young.

37

GUARDING THE NEST

Guard bees at the nest entrance try to detect and sting invaders before they can get in. When a bee stings, it releases a scent that signals other bees to join in the fight. If an invader manages to pass the guards, the first bee to find it in the nest will try to kill it, and others will quickly come to help.

Ants often invade bees' nests to steal honey. Since they are too small for stinging, the bees pick them up in their jaws, carry

Worker bees surround and attack an invading bumblebee on the wall of the comb. The worker to the left of the bumblebee is stinging the intruder, which is very unlikely to survive.

them out alive, and drop them a safe distance away from the nest.

The biggest insects that attack bees' nests are hornets. These are large wasps that wait outside a nest and carry off workers to a nearby tree to eat. If bees can catch a hornet, they crowd around, stinging and smothering it, until the hornet suffocates and dies.

HITCHHIKING BEETLES

The tiny **larva** of the oil beetle is an enemy of **burrowing** bees such as mining bees. It waits in a flower until a burrowing bee comes to collect nectar. Then it climbs onto the bee and hitches a ride back to its nest, where it feeds on the bee's eggs and later eats the stored honey.

Show Me the Way

In Africa there is a bird called the honey-guide that is very fond of eating bee larvae, but is not strong enough to break into a bees' nest. Other animals that like honey, including humans, have learned to follow the honey-guide as it flies. It calls loudly as it leads its followers to a nest it has discovered. When the larger animal has broken into the bees' nest, the honey-guide feasts on the larvae and the wax **comb** left behind. This honey-guide is feeding on a broken piece of comb left for it as a thank-you gift by the humans whom it led to the bees' nest.

I DIDN'T KNOW THAT

CHAPTER 8
Humans and Honey

Bees are the only insect that can produce food eaten by humans.

The ancient Egyptians kept bees and traded honey along the coast of East Africa thousands of years ago.

A group of beehives is called an apiary, and a person who works with bees is called an apiarist.

The ancient Mayans of Mexico worshiped gods that looked like bees.

Widespread spraying of pesticides kills bees and threatens not only honey production but also many fruit crops.

▶ This cutaway picture shows the arrangement of frames inside a typical modern hive. The beekeeper removes the frames in the upper section to extract the honey.

The first people to taste honey must have raided wild bees' nests. One day, someone probably cut off the branch containing the nest and took it home. This was the beginning of beekeeping, and led to the invention of the modern hive, or artificial nest.

A BOX OF BEES

When a **swarm** of honeybees is put into a hive containing wax sheets on which their **cells** can be built, the bees will settle down and get to work making their nest there.

Honey is stored in the upper chamber

Honeybee larvae grow in the lower chamber

Hive entrance

Until fairly recently, bees kept by humans were housed in dome-shaped baskets called skeps. Modern hives, however, are made in square wooden sections, with an upper chamber where the bees store the honey, just as they do in the wild, and a lower chamber where they keep the young and the **pollen.** The upper chamber contains frames that can be removed when they are full to extract the honey.

Commercial beekeepers can get as much as 80 pounds (40 kilograms) of honey and 1 pound (0.5 kilogram) of beeswax from each of their hives every year. Because so much of the bees' honey is removed, the beekeeper gives each colony some sugary syrup to eat over the winter months. Some beekeepers have thousands of hives.

OTHER HONEY-MAKERS

Today, most beekeepers use European honeybees, also known as common honeybees. No honeybees existed in North and South America at all until they were brought by European colonists. Native peoples in tropical regions, such as near the Amazon in South America, kept

Wearing a hat and veil to keep him safe from stings, a beekeeper checks on his bees in the hive. He calms the bees first by gently puffing smoke into the hive.

stingless bees for their honey. The honeybees brought by the Europeans never adapted well to warmer climates in the Americas, so beekeepers brought a type of honey-producing bee from Africa called the killer bee. It is not more poisonous than other bees, but it will attack in large numbers if disturbed. Such an attack can be deadly to humans and animals.

ENEMIES OF THE BEEKEEPER

The most threatening enemy to hive bees in Europe and North and South America is the varroa mite, which can kill whole colonies by sucking blood from the bees until they are too weak to go out to find food. The mite came from the Far East, where local bees are not harmed by it because they know how to groom each other to get rid of the mites. However, bees cannot do this in other parts of the world. Beekeepers use formic acid, produced naturally by ants, to kill these serious pests.

THE FRUIT-MAKERS

Pollinating flowers is by far the most important function of bees.

Hives in a meadow of heather flowers produce delicious heather honey. To make honey with a particular flavor, beekeepers put their hives where there are many flowers of the same kind.

Pollinated flowers produce fruits such as beans, apples, pears, and tomatoes—all important crops—as well as seeds for next year's plants. Beekeepers earn part of their income by taking their bees to orchards and farms, often many miles away, where the bees can work all spring to pollinate the flowers while they make honey—and money—for their keeper. A world without bees would be a world without colorful flowering plants and delicious fruits and honey.

BEE PRODUCTS

Humans have found a wide range of uses for things made by bees. Beeswax is used in candles, furniture polish, and cosmetics, and honey is widely used as a natural food sweetener and flavoring. Because the fruit sugars in honey are easily digested by humans, honey is often eaten by athletes to help give them extra energy when they perform.

Healing Bees

Bees and their honey are used in many medical treatments for humans. Beestings contain a substance that is sometimes used in the treatment of diseases like rheumatism and arthritis. Some people allow bees to sting them because it eases the pain in their aching joints. In Europe, the poison produced by a particular kind of bee is used in an ointment to warm up and loosen stiff muscles.

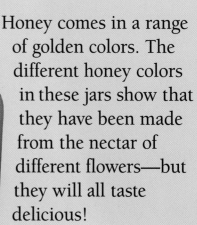

Honey has long been used in medicines for stomachaches and hay fever. Since it is also widely believed to kill germs, honey is sometimes used in the treatment of wounds and sore throats.

Honey comes in a range of golden colors. The different honey colors in these jars show that they have been made from the nectar of different flowers—but they will all taste delicious!

Glossary

abdomen rear section of an insect's body

antenna (more than one are called antennae) feelers on an insect's head, used for touching and detecting tastes, smells, sounds, and motion

anther male part of a flower that produces pollen

burrow to dig a hole or tunnel. A hole or tunnel used by an animal as a home or nest is also called a burrow.

cell one of many thousands of small, six-sided wax chambers in a comb, in which honeybees store honey and pollen and raise their young

chitin substance that forms a bee's wings

color spectrum all the colors of light, including many that are invisible to humans

comb collection of wax cells that make up a honeybee nest

compound eye eye made up of hundreds or thousands of tiny lenses and found mainly in adult insects

drone male member of a bee colony

evaporate to change water from a liquid into vapor

evolve to develop slowly over time

fertilized in an egg, to have joined together the female and male sex cell so that a new organism can develop

forage to search for food. A forager is a worker honeybee that leaves the nest to search for food.

gland organ that produces substances an animal needs

hibernate to spend the winter in a special kind of deep sleep

honey stomach organ used to store and carry nectar and water, located in front of the true stomach in a honeybee's abdomen

larva (more than one are called larvae) second, wormlike stage in the life cycle of many insects

metamorphosis complete change in form that some animals (such as bees, frogs, and butterflies) go through to become adults

paralyze to cause to be unable to move

pollen dustlike grains produced by a flower for reproduction purposes

pollinate to carry pollen from the male part of a flower to the female part, allowing it to produce a seed. This process is called pollination.

prey animal that is hunted by other animals for food

propolis substance produced by the buds of trees and collected by honeybees

pupa (more than one are called pupae) third stage in the life cycle of most insects in which the young insect develops into the adult form inside a hard protective case.

queen substance chemical released by the queen in a bee colony that ensures no other queen will be born, and that keeps all the other bees doing the jobs needed for the survival of the colony

regurgitate to bring something back up through the mouth that has been swallowed; to vomit

reproduction process of having offspring

royal jelly special food produced by worker honeybees and fed to larvae for the first three days of their lives. Queens eat it throughout their lives.

social living in groups that work together

species group of organisms that share certain features and that can breed together to produce offspring that can also breed

swarm large group of worker honeybees leaving a crowded nest to start a new nest with the queen

stigma female part of a flower that contains eggs and where seeds form

thorax middle part of an insect's body containing muscles that move the wings and legs

ultraviolet kind of light that humans cannot see, but bees and many other insects can

Further Reading

Cole, Joanna. *The Magic School Bus Inside a Beehive.* Illustrated by Bruce Degen. New York: Scholastic, 1998.

Facklam, Margery. *Bees Dance and Whales Sing: The Mysteries of Animal Communication.* Illustrated by Pamela Johnson. San Francisco: Sierra Club, 2001.

Facklam, Margery. *What's the Buzz? The Secret Lives of Bees.* Chicago: Raintree, 1999.

Furgang, Kathy. *Let's Take a Trip to a Beehive.* New York: Rosen, 2000.

Kalman, Bobbie. *Hooray for Beekeeping!* New York: Crabtree, 1997.

Robinson, W. Wright. *How Insects Build Their Amazing Homes.* Farmington Hills, Mich.: Blackbirch Press, 1999.

Swan Miller, Sara. *Ants, Bees, and Wasps of North America.* Danbury, Conn.: Scholastic Library, 2003.

Index